494

my

N.E.

7109

Free Speech

Identifying Propaganda Techniques

Curriculum Consultant: JoAnne Buggey, Ph.D.
College of Education, University of Minnesota

By Bradley Steffens

Greenhaven Press, Inc.
Post Office Box 289009
San Diego, CA 92198-9009

Titles in the opposing viewpoints juniors series:

Advertising
AIDS
Alcohol
Animal Rights
Causes of Crime
Child Abuse
Christopher Columbus
Death Penalty
Drugs and Sports
Elections
Endangered Species

The Environment
Forests
Free Speech
Garbage
Gun Control
The Homeless
Immigration
Nuclear Power
The Palestinian Conflict
Patriotism
Pollution

Population
Poverty
Prisons
Smoking
Television
Toxic Wastes
The U.S. Constitution
The War on Drugs
Working Mothers
Zoos

Cover photo: © 1989/T.L. Litt/Impact Visuals

Library of Congress Cataloging-in-Publication Data

Steffens, Bradley, 1956-
   Free speech : identifying propaganda techniques / by Bradley
Steffens ; curriculum consultant, JoAnne Buggey.
   p. c.m. — (Opposing viewpoints juniors)
   Includes bibliographical references and index.
   Summary: Presents opposing viewpoints on topics related to free
speech, accompanied by critical thinking activities to help the
reader discern fact from opinion and recognize propaganda
techniques.
   ISBN 0-89908-098-7 (alk. paper)
   1. Freedom of speech—Juvenile literature. 2. Propaganda—
Juvenile literature. [1. Freedom of speech. 2. Propaganda.
3. Critical thinking.] I. Title. II. Series.
JC591.S74 1992
323.44'3—dc20   92-23594
                                                            CIP
                                                            AC

CONTENTS

An Introduction to Opposing Viewpoints

When people disagree, it is hard to figure out who is right. You may decide one person is right just because the person is your friend or a relative. But this is not a very good reason to agree or disagree with someone. It is better if you try to understand why these people disagree. On what main points do they differ? Read or listen to each person's argument carefully. Separate the facts and opinions that each person presents. Finally, decide which argument best matches what you think. This process, examining an argument without emotion, is part of what critical thinking is all about.

This is not easy. Many things make it hard to understand and form opinions. People's values, ages, and experiences all influence the way they think. This is why learning to read and think critically is an invaluable skill. Opposing Viewpoints Juniors books will help you learn and practice skills to improve your ability to read critically. By reading opposing views on an issue, you will become familiar with methods people use to attempt to convince you that their point of view is right. And you will learn to separate the authors' opinions from the facts they present.

Each Opposing Viewpoints Juniors book focuses on one critical thinking skill that will help you judge the views presented. Some of these skills are telling fact from opinion, recognizing propaganda techniques, and locating and analyzing the main idea. These skills will allow you to examine opposing viewpoints more easily.

What Are Propaganda Techniques?

Propaganda is information presented in an attempt to influence people. In this Opposing Viewpoints Juniors book you will be asked to identify and study several common propaganda techniques. Some of these techniques appeal to your ability to think logically while others appeal to your emotions.

All propaganda techniques distract the listener or reader from the complete picture. People who use propaganda techniques encourage you to look only at the factors that are important to accepting their argument as true. The propaganda will be offered as a reason to believe the argument, but in reality will be weak, distracting, or irrelevant reasons. Some of these persuasive techniques may be relevant to your decision to agree or not, but others will not be. It is important to sift through the information, weeding the false reasoning from the proof.

While there are many types of propaganda techniques, this book will focus on three of them. These are *testimonial, generalization,* and *scare tactics.* Examples of these techniques are given below:

Testimonial—quoting or paraphrasing an authority or celebrity to support one's own argument. Often, the celebrity is not qualified to express an opinion on the subject. For example, movie stars are often used to recommend a product they may know nothing about.

Testimonials can be used in a positive way as well. If the person quoted is truly an authority on the subject being talked about, the testimonial can support an argument. Quoting comedian Richard Pryor about how drugs almost ruined his life is an example of a testimonial that presents a legitimate reason to believe drugs can be dangerous. Pryor *is* an authority on this subject and can give advice based on his personal experience.

Generalization—a statement that suggests that all members of a group are the same in some way. A generalization denies that some members of the group may be different. For example, the statement "Truck drivers listen to country music" implies that all truck drivers listen to country music when, in fact, some truck drivers may never do so.

Generalizations can also apply to places and things. For example, "The world's beaches are polluted with plastic debris" is a generalization. It implies that all beaches everywhere are littered with plastic. But many are not.

People who use generalizations often cite an example in which the situation is true in one instance to convince you that it is true all the time. For example, a person may say, "Teenagers are careless drivers. This morning I saw a teenager flip his car, injuring himself and his passengers." The speaker hopes to convince you that because one teenager drove carelessly, all teenagers do.

Scare tactics—the threat that if you do not do or believe this, something terrible will happen. People using this technique write or say alarming words and phrases to persuade you to believe their argument.

An example is "Illegal immigration endangers every worker in the United States." The person quoted does not say *how* illegal immigration will endanger everyone. The purpose of the statement is to scare you into believing his argument. The person wants you to make a decision based on fear about the issue, not on logical reasoning.

When reading differing arguments, then, there is a lot to think about. Are the authors giving sound reasons for their points of view? Or do they distort the importance of their arguments with generalizations, use testimonials deceptively, or play on your fear and emotions through scare tactics?

We asked two students to give their opinions on free speech. Look for examples of testimonial, generalization, and scare tactics in their arguments.

People should not be able to say anything they want to.

"Sticks and stones may break my bones, but words will never hurt me," goes the nursery rhyme, but it is not true. Words can hurt people, and they often do. Telling a person a lie about someone else is bad, but telling a lie on radio or TV about an important person can ruin that person's career. That is why we have laws that protect people against lies told in public. They are known as slander laws.

Slander is not the only kind of harmful speech. Yelling "Fire" in a crowded theater is dangerous. False advertising can cause people to waste money on products that do not work. Dirty language upsets some people deeply. Many kinds of speech can be harmful. That is why we have laws that keep people from saying anything they want.

Free speech is not total. There are bad people in the world, and bad people will use speech to do bad things. For example, the singer Ice-T wrote a song called "Cop Killer." In the song, Ice-T calls the police "pigs." He sings, "Got my shotgun sawed off . . . 'Bout to dust some cops off . . . Die, Pig, Die." Kids who listen to this song might think it is okay to kill cops. This puts the lives of police officers in danger. I think that Ice-T shouldn't be allowed to put songs like that on his record.

People should be able to say anything they want to.

My dad always says, "If something doesn't kill you, it only makes you stronger." That's how I feel about things people say. If you listen to something someone says and disagree with it, or even hate it, it doesn't kill you. It only makes you stronger.

Words are just words. You don't have to listen to them. You can ignore them. If you do listen to them, you can use your mind to think about them and reject them. Someone might say, "Hey, you should kill a cop." That doesn't mean you have to go out and do it. People can think for themselves.

That's why we don't need laws about speech. People can handle ugly, awful speech. The real danger lies in making laws that limit speech. These laws can be used to shut people up, even when they have something worthwhile to say. Once the government has the power to silence some speech, it can use that power to silence more speech, and finally all speech. The danger of government controlling speech is greater than the danger of people saying things that might hurt someone.

Roger and Gail have very different opinions about free speech. Both use examples of propaganda techniques in their arguments.

Roger:

GENERALIZATION

There are bad people in the world, and bad people will use speech to do bad things.

SCARE TACTIC

Kids who listen to this song might think it is okay to kill cops. This puts the lives of police officers in danger.

TESTIMONIAL

Ice-T calls the police "pigs." He sings, "Got my shotgun sawed off . . . 'Bout to dust some cops off . . . Die, Pig, Die."

Gail:

GENERALIZATION

People can handle ugly, awful speech.

SCARE TACTIC

Once the government has the power to silence some speech, it can use that power to silence more speech, and finally all speech.

TESTIMONIAL

My dad always says, "If something doesn't kill you, it only makes you stronger."

In this sample, Roger and Gail use some propaganda techniques when presenting their opinions. Both Roger and Gail think they are right about free speech. What do you conclude about free speech from this sample? Why?

As you continue to read through the viewpoints in this book, try keeping a tally like the one above to compare the authors' arguments.

CHAPTER 1

PREFACE: Should There Be Limits to Free Speech?

Should there be limits to free speech? Many Americans would answer no to this question. Freedom of expression is one of the basic privileges bestowed on all Americans by the Bill of Rights, the first ten amendments to the Constitution. Traditionally, no form of expression can be censored unless it poses a direct harm to others.

But the question inevitably arises regarding the kinds of harm from which people should be protected: From racists who preach hatred and encourage violence? From anarchists who advocate an end to legitimate government? From people or organizations that promote harmful products or vividly portray sex or violence in the public media? From recording artists who promote ideas such as committing suicide or killing people?

While some Americans believe that the public should be protected from all of these things, others say that such protections are merely forms of censorship. Preventing an anarchist from preaching revolution is one step toward censoring *all* unpopular kinds of expression. The viewpoints that follow debate the limits of free speech. Watch for the use of testimonials, scare tactics, and generalizations in the arguments.

Editor's Note: The author of this viewpoint argues that government exists to secure individual rights. Since, in the author's opinion, laws that limit speech violate the right to free speech, the author believes that such laws should be struck down. Does the author use generalizations, testimonials, or scare tactics to persuade you?

The first sentence of this viewpoint makes the generalization that the founders of the United States were very wise. It is intended to make the reader feel good about what the author has to say.

The author quotes Thomas Jefferson to support his argument. The author's use of this quote is legitimate, because Jefferson was a key thinker about the role of government in people's lives.

The people who founded this country were very wise. When they broke away from British rule, they wrote down their reasons for doing so. They thought long and hard about the purpose of government. They chose their words carefully.

The wisest of our nation's founders, Thomas Jefferson, believed that the only reason to have a government was to protect individual rights. "All men . . . are endowed by their Creator with certain unalienable rights," he wrote in the Declaration of Independence, "that to secure these rights, governments are instituted among men." Jefferson and the other founders knew that government should protect individual citizens' rights at all costs.

One of the rights the government protects is the right to free speech. Some people keep trying to limit this right by arguing for laws to censor the speech of others. These people have forgotten that government exists to enforce people's rights, not to take their rights away. When people try to take away the right to free speech, they strike at the very heart of why our government exists in the first place: to secure individual rights.

"WELL IF YOU ASK ME, THE FIRST AMENDMENT SHOULD ONLY PROTECT UNCONTROVERSIAL EXPRESSION."

Jim Borgman. Reprinted with special permission of King Features Syndicate, Inc.

Even offensive or hateful speech should not be outlawed. Hurt feelings or even disgust at what is being said are not reasons to limit speech. As U.S. Supreme Court justice William Brennan put it, "If there is a bedrock principle underlying the First Amendment, it is that the government may not prohibit the expression of an idea simply because society finds the idea offensive or disagreeable."

Hate crime laws also endanger free speech. These laws allow the government to punish people if they attack someone's race or religion, such as by burning a cross or painting a swastika on a building. Such actions are clearly offensive, but still should not be outlawed. In 1992, the U.S. Supreme Court struck down a St. Paul, Minnesota, hate crime law because, as Justice Antonin Scalia put it, the First Amendment forbids "silencing speech on the basis of its content." Although the St. Paul law was struck down, other cities and states still have hate crime laws that remain in force. These must be struck down as well.

Free speech can lead to unpleasant and even offensive things being said. Although this is frustrating, we must accept it. The law must be applied fairly to everyone. If we allow exceptions for speech that is offensive, it will be harder to defend legitimate political protest and dissent. Too many exceptions would damage the First Amendment and endanger the nation by opening the door for government to put people in prison for saying the wrong thing.

The author quotes a Supreme Court justice to support his argument. This quote is relevant because justices are the ones that must decide many cases involving free speech.

The author quotes a recent ruling by the Supreme Court. This is a relevant testimonial, because the Supreme Court must decide whether laws that conflict with the First Amendment are constitutional.

The author suggests that scary things will happen if exceptions to the First Amendment are allowed. This is a scare tactic, because the author does not say how these things will occur.

Individual rights

The author argues that the purpose of government is to secure individual rights. Do you agree or disagree? Why? What other purposes could government have? Explain.

Editor's Note: The author of this viewpoint argues that harmful speech should be limited. As you read, be aware of how the author attempts to persuade you. Take note of which propaganda techniques are used.

The author generalizes about the power of words. This generalization has little to do with the issue of free speech.

The author quotes John Locke to support his point. This testimonial is relevant, since Locke influenced the thinking of the authors of the U.S. Constitution.

The author generalizes about those who call for free speech. He suggests that they all think alike. This generalization is really a personal attack on those with whom the author disagrees.

The author describes many things that would occur if there were no limits on speech. This is a scare tactic.

Words are powerful. Handled with skill, they can express our deepest thoughts and feelings about ourselves and the world around us. But words can also be used to arouse anger, to degrade people, and to destroy lives. It all depends upon the person using the words.

Without limits on speech, dangerous situations can occur. For example, words can be used to incite a crowd to acts of violence: Adolf Hitler's speeches caused his followers to attack and kill Jews. Words spoken at Ku Klux Klan rallies have led crowds to lynch black people. In such cases, the actions of the mobs were wrong, but so were the speeches that gave the mobs focus and direction. Such harmful forms of speech must be outlawed.

Speech must be limited for the same reason that any other human activity must be limited: to prevent harm. When there are no rules or laws to govern conduct, people will simply do as they please, and the strongest will victimize the weakest.

The great English philosopher John Locke called life without laws or limits the "state of nature." In this state of nature, Locke said, everyone has individual rights, but the ability to enjoy these rights "is very uncertain and constantly exposed to the invasion of others." To protect their rights, people band together to form a society. They enter into what Locke called a social "compact" with other people. They agree to give up some of their individual freedom in return for greater security for their natural rights. They replace the rule of might with the rule of law.

Those who want to remove all limits on speech have forgotten about this social compact. They place individual rights above the common good. They wish people to speak with total freedom, as if they lived in the state of nature rather than in civil society.

If we were to dissolve the limits on speech, people could say anything they want. Politicians could lie about their opponents. Newspapers could defame their critics. Advertisers could make false claims about their products. Thugs could urge crowds to commit violent acts, without fear of going to jail. Unlimited freedom of speech would create chaos.

Ed Gamble. Reprinted with permission.

These dangers are real. All of the examples mentioned above have happened, and laws have been written to keep them from happening again. Slander laws prohibit speakers from telling damaging lies about others. Libel laws keep publishers from printing similar falsehoods. Laws against false and deceptive advertising keep advertisers from making untrue claims about their products. Incitement laws stop speakers from urging others to lawless action.

The U.S. Supreme Court, which decides the meaning of the First Amendment, has already ruled that these and other laws that limit speech are just and constitutional. It is true that these rulings take away some individual liberty, but this is the price we pay for living in society. As Supreme Court justice Robert H. Jackson put it in 1949 in an important free speech case, *Terminiello v. Chicago*, "The choice is not between law and order and liberty. It is between liberty with order and anarchy without either." To live together in a civilized society, we must accept certain limits on our behavior.

The author points out that the scary things described in the preceding paragraph have actually happened in the past. This makes his claim less of a scare tactic.

The author quotes a Supreme Court justice to support his point. This testimonial is relevant, because the Supreme Court interprets the First Amendment.

The common good

The author argues that people must give up some of their individual rights to form a society for the common good. Do you agree? Why or why not? Should free speech be one of the rights people give up? Why or why not?

CRITICAL THINKING SKILL 1

Identifying Propaganda Techniques

After reading the two viewpoints on free speech, make a chart similar to the one made for Gail and Roger on page 8. List one example of each propaganda technique from each viewpoint. A chart is started for you below:

Viewpoint 1:

TESTIMONIAL

"All men . . . are endowed by their Creator with certain unalienable rights," he wrote in the Declaration of Independence, "that to secure these rights, governments are instituted among men."

GENERALIZATION

The people who founded this country were very wise.

Viewpoint 2:

SCARE TACTIC

Unlimited freedom of speech would create chaos.

GENERALIZATION

Those who want to remove all limits on speech have forgotten about the social compact.

After completing your chart, answer the following questions:

Which article used the most propaganda techniques?
Which argument was the most convincing? Why?

PREFACE: Should Freedom of the Press Be Limited?

The First Amendment contains just eleven words about freedom of the press, but millions more have been written about what that freedom includes. News reporters and publishers think that the interpretation of the First Amendment should be broad. They believe that the public has the right to any information as long as it is true. It does not matter, they say, if this information embarrasses a person, lets a government secret be known, or even provides information that might encourage lawless action. For example, in 1979 *The Progressive* magazine published a Princeton undergraduate's crude, but workable plans for building a nuclear bomb. Although this information could aid terrorists attempting to build a nuclear weapon, members of the press defended the magazine's right to publish it.

Critics of the news media disagree. They argue that restraints are needed to protect the rights of individuals and preserve society as a whole. For example, in 1991, NBC News broadcast the name of the woman who had accused William Kennedy Smith, a member of the Kennedy family, of rape. Although the information was true, critics say it violated the woman's right to privacy. Critics also point out that the news media can and do make mistakes and should be held accountable when they do.

In the following viewpoints, the author debates the merits of a free press. Look for examples of testimonials, generalizations, and scare tactics.

Editor's Note: The author of this viewpoint argues that the press must enjoy complete freedom if it is to keep the public informed. Find the propaganda techniques the author uses to support his ideas.

The author quotes Thomas Jefferson. Is this testimonial relevant or is it a propaganda technique? Give reasons to support your answer.

The author makes a statement about all political leaders. What propaganda technique is this?

This paragraph begins with a propaganda technique. Which one is it? How can you tell?

Mario Cuomo is a government official. Is his testimonial relevant, or is it a propaganda technique? Explain.

"Were it left to me to decide whether we should have a government without newspapers, or newspapers without government, I should not hesitate to choose the latter," wrote Thomas Jefferson, the third president of the United States and author of the Declaration of Independence. His view sums up why the founders of our nation made freedom of the press the very first protection listed in the Bill of Rights. Without newspapers to report on the actions and misdeeds of government, political leaders always abuse their power. The founders had lived under one harsh government. They did not want to create another. They believed that a free press would serve as a watchdog and prevent abuses of power.

The United States is the greatest country in the world, and a free press is one of the chief reasons it is. As Mario Cuomo, governor of New York, puts it, "The more I learn about government and especially about democracy, the more deeply convinced I become that one of our greatest strengths as a people is our right to full and free expression. No people have benefited more from the gift of free speech and a free press."

"WE'D BETTER TONE THIS DOWN OR GEORGE III WILL SUE US FOR LIBEL..."

Tony Auth © 1985, Washington Post Writers Group, reprinted with permission.

A free press is especially vital for a democracy, where the people rule themselves by choosing their leaders. To make these choices, the people need to know what their leaders are doing. The press provides this information. Any attempt to limit the press conflicts with the people's "right to know." It is also the first step toward controlling what the people think.

If a government controls the facts newspapers print, it also controls people's opinions. After all, a person cannot form an opinion critical of a government if that person does not know what evil and deceptive actions government may be planning. As syndicated columnist David S. Broder argues, "Control of information gives a government control over its citizens' minds."

This is why the framers of the Constitution defined freedom of the press in such sweeping terms. They could have added limits or exceptions to the First Amendment, but they chose not to do so. Instead they wrote that "Congress shall make no law abridging . . . freedom of the press." Their intention could not have been clearer. U.S. Supreme Court justice William Brennan in 1957 stated bluntly in *Roth v. United States*, "I read *no law abridging* to mean NO LAW ABRIDGING."

It is in our own best interest to protect the First Amendment from those who would strip it of its power. Otherwise, we will end up with a government that will control not only what we read but what we say and even what we think. Once that happens, it will be too late to go back.

When an author uses a term like *any* it often signals the use of a propaganda technique. Is this the case here?

The author quotes Supreme Court justice Brennan. In the case cited, the majority of the court did not agree with Justice Brennan. Does this fact strengthen, weaken, or have any effect on the use of his quote as a testimonial?

The author concludes with a statement about the future. Which propaganda technique is this?

"Americans have grown so much happier since we eliminated the free press."

Don Wright/*The Miami News*. Reprinted with permission.

Dangerous leaders

The author states that without newspapers to report on their actions, leaders will abuse their power. Do you agree or disagree? How else are the country's leaders controlled?

Editor's Note: The author argues that the press is endangering the U.S. government and the public by reporting government secrets and other information irresponsibly. Which propaganda techniques does he use to support his argument?

Which propaganda technique is used at the beginning of this viewpoint? How can you tell?

This paragraph includes several sentences that use the same propaganda technique. Which one is it?

Are these examples realistic, or are they scare tactics? Why?

WHAT IF TODAY'S MEDIA HAD BEEN THERE IN 1775...

SO IT'LL BE ONE IF BY LAND, TWO IF BY SEA! BACK TO YOU, TOM.

Steve Kelley. Reprinted with permission.

The author quotes a journalist to support his point about the press. Is this an effective testimonial? Why or why not?

When the founders guaranteed freedom of the press under the Bill of Rights, they did not foresee how large and powerful the press would become. In fact, the term *the press* is not even accurate anymore. The most powerful portions of what we call the press—television and radio—do not even use printing presses.

This difference is important for several reasons. First, people today are much more exposed to the news. Television and radio broadcast it right into their homes. Most people no longer read the news and think about it. Instead, the news is read to them, and news analysts tell them what it means. Today's news organizations are much larger than any newspaper that existed when the Constitution was written. They are also much more powerful.

Because of these changes, the news media can do much more damage than ever before. A public figure can be ruined overnight by a hostile news story, even if it is not true. During war, a leader can learn about the movements of the enemy from the television news faster than he can from the battlefield itself. The news now moves with twentieth-century speed. It is silly to think it can be governed by eighteenth-century standards.

The Supreme Court has ruled that the press can be kept from printing news in which the government has "a compelling interest." During World War II, the United States broke the Japanese secret code. This meant that the United States could anticipate and repel Japanese attacks. A reporter learned of the breakthrough and reported it. When the Japanese heard of the report, they changed their code. Thousands of Americans lost their lives because the press "spilled the beans" about the code. If the press could be trusted with military and government secrets, it would not have to be restricted. But the press has forfeited this trust.

Members of the press counter this criticism by saying that even when they steal secrets, they are acting on behalf of "the people's right to know." They see themselves as "watchdogs" of the government. For example, in 1984 the *Washington Post* published details of a secret satellite launched by the U.S. Air Force, even though the secretary of defense had asked that they not do so. Patrick J. Buchanan, a journalist, explains what is wrong with this reasoning: "The American people were not clamoring to know the purposes, capabilities, and launch details of this satellite the Air Force is sending up to advance national security." The "people's right to know" is a handy excuse the press uses to pry into government secrets.

When asked why he chose to ignore the government request not to publish details about the satellite, the editor of the *Washington Post*, Benjamin Bradlee, replied, "We listen and we decide what to do." In other words, Bradlee believes that the press, not the government, should have the final say about national security matters. When the press can make national security decisions that affect the rest of us, it has become too powerful.

The government is not the enemy of the people, as the press believes. The government serves the people. John C. Merrill, a former reporter who now teaches journalism, writes, "The press should remember that, after all, the people at least elect government officials (or some of them); the people never elect an editor, an anchorperson, a news director, a publisher, or a reporter."

The press is big business. It is too big and powerful to be trusted with limiting itself. If the power of the press is not curbed, more and more people will be hurt, and the government itself will be crippled. A weakened government will not be able to protect any of our rights. If the press gets its way, it will destroy the freedoms we all enjoy.

> Which propaganda technique is used in this paragraph?

> Is this an effective testimonial? Why or why not?

> The viewpoint concludes with a propaganda technique. Which one is it?

Steve Kelley. Reprinted with permission.

Dangerous press

The author states that without limits on the press, the news media will hurt people and cripple the government. Do you agree or disagree? Other than through laws, how can the power of the media be curbed?

FREE SPEECH **19**

Identifying Propaganda Techniques

This activity will allow you to practice identifying two of the propaganda techniques you have been learning about in this book. The statements below focus on the subject matter of this book—whether there should be limits on free speech. *Mark an S for any statement you believe is an example of scare tactics, T for any statement that is a testimonial, and N for a statement that is neither.*

If you are doing this activity as a member of a class or group, compare your answer with other class or group members. You may find that others have answers different from yours. Listening to the reasons others give for their answers can help you in identifying propaganda techniques.

EXAMPLE: "Were it left to me to decide whether we should have a government without newspapers, or newspapers without government, I should not hesitate to choose the latter," wrote Thomas Jefferson, the third president of the United States and author of the Declaration of Independence.

ANSWER: T, testimonial. The author is using the words of Thomas Jefferson to support his argument.

Answer

1. As Mario Cuomo, governor of New York, argues, "The more I learn about government and especially about democracy, the more deeply convinced I become that one of our greatest strengths as a people is our right to full and free expression." _____

2. Any attempt to limit the press conflicts with the people's "right to know." It is also the first step toward controlling what the people think. _____

3. If a government controls the facts newspapers print, it also controls people's opinions. _____

4. Justice William Brennan in 1957 stated bluntly in *Roth v. United States*, "I read *no law abridging* to mean NO LAW ABRIDGING." _____

5. If the press could be trusted with military and government secrets, it would not have to be restricted. _____

6. If the power of the press is not curbed, more and more people will be hurt, and government itself will be crippled. _____

7. A weakened government will not be able to protect any of our rights. If the press gets its way, it will destroy the freedoms we all enjoy. _____

CHAPTER 3

PREFACE: Is Library Censorship Justified?

Should children and the general public be protected from books and pamphlets that might be considered harmful? Some people answer this question in the affirmative: Since choices must be made anyway, librarians should choose only materials that reflect the values of the majority. Others answer this question in the negative: Since libraries are part of a democratic government, materials should reflect the full range of opinions and tastes, not just those of the majority.

The last few years have seen increasing pressure on public libraries to ban certain books. Some pressure comes from parents who do not want their children exposed to ideas and values that conflict with their religious beliefs. For example, parents in Yorba Linda, California, asked that Maurice Sendak's book *Where the Wild Things Are* be removed from the school library because they believed it promoted "Satanism." Other pressure comes from racial groups that object to how members of their race are portrayed. David Perry, a city-councilperson in Plano, Texas, objects to the presence of Mark Twain's novel *Huckleberry Finn* on school reading lists because it contains racist language and attitudes.

The authors in the following viewpoints debate the issue of whether certain materials should be banned from libraries. Each author uses testimonials. Evaluate the testimonials carefully. Are the testimonials relevant to the author's arguments? Or are they distracting and irrelevant?

Editor's Note: In this viewpoint, the author argues that the public, not librarians, should have the final say about what books are included in libraries.

According to the Library of Congress, thousands of new books are published each year. Most librarians only have enough shelf space and money to acquire a tiny portion of these books. They select these few books carefully. They do not choose books by alphabetical order, by price alone, or by any other arbitrary system. They decide which books to order based on the contents of each book—its subject matter, its quality, its reputation, and whether it would benefit library patrons. Other books are excluded on the same basis. Because the librarian makes the decisions about which books will be available to library patrons, this selection process could be called censorship. However, few people object to this practice.

Since librarians must limit their selections anyway, they should try to include only the very best books. Books that degrade people, make

Chuck Asay by permission of the *Colorado Springs Gazette Telegraph.*

fun of religious beliefs, contain offensive language, or are especially violent should be rejected. Perhaps some books that include these things are worthwhile, but why bother to include them when there are equally good books that are much less offensive?

When librarians order books, they do not pay for them with their own money. They spend the public's money. Like all other agents of government, librarians must account for how they spend the public money. As author and activist Phyllis Schlafly states, "The public has the right to exercise its right of free speech and on how taxpayers' funds are spent and on what standards, to second-guess the judgement of the persons doing the spending, and to remove from office those responsible for any misuse of tax money." Schlafly's suggested course of action is not censorship. It is democracy.

Most taxpayers are very tolerant of new and unusual ideas. But ideas are one thing and offensiveness is something else. A person of color should not have to fund the purchase of a book that contains racist remarks and language. A woman should not have to accept the presence of a book, record, or video that encourages hatred of women. Andrea Dworkin, a feminist author, says, "There are lots of people in this country, I am happy to say, who . . . will not accept the hatred of women as good, wholesome, American fun; they won't accept the hatred of women . . . as anybody's idea of freedom." Offensive books cannot be banned from private bookstores, but they can and should be banned from public libraries.

The least that librarians can do is to show respect for the beliefs and values of the people who pay their salaries. If librarians fail to respond to the concerns of the public, they should not be surprised if the public reacts by cutting their funding and forcing libraries to close. The librarians will have lost the very thing they tried to protect. They will have no one to blame but themselves.

Is the author's statement about librarians a generalization? Why or why not?

The author quotes Phyllis Schlafly. Is this testimonial effective? Explain.

What propaganda technique does the author use at the beginning of this paragraph?

The author quotes Andrea Dworkin. Does this testimonial support his argument? Why or why not?

Which propaganda technique does the author use at the end of this viewpoint?

A public issue?

The author states that librarians must be accountable to the public for the use of public money. Do you agree or disagree? Should librarians be free to buy any books they want? Why or why not?

Editor's Note: The author of this viewpoint maintains that public libraries should carry a broad range of materials. Watch for the use of propaganda techniques as you read.

The author talks about several groups of people in broad terms. Which propaganda technique is this? Why?

Freedom of the press does not mean anything unless it is accompanied by a freedom to read. If a book cannot be found in the library, it may as well not have been printed at all. Unfortunately, many good books are missing from library collections today because a few people have pressured librarians into removing them. The People for the American Way, a group that monitors censorship cases, reported in its annual report that there were 244 incidents of attempted book bannings in 39 states.

The pressure to ban certain books from libraries does not come from just one group. Christians say libraries should not carry books about the devil and witchcraft. African-Americans object to books like *Little Black Sambo* and *Huckleberry Finn* because these books include racist words and attitudes. Even the *American Heritage Dictionary* has been removed from some schools and libraries because it defines slang terms for sex. The works of John Steinbeck, Ernest Hemingway, Anne Frank, Alice Walker, Judy Blume, and J.D. Salinger have been banned as well.

Every time one group succeeds in banning a book, another group is encouraged to do the same. Pretty soon, library shelves will be empty. The free flow of ideas will trickle to a stop.

P.S. Mueller

MEET ME AT THE BOOK-BURNING!!

© 1986 BY P.S. MUELLER

I'LL BE THE LIBERAL WITH A COPY OF TWAIN.

AND YOU'LL BE THE CONSERVATIVE WITH PLANNED PARENTHOOD PAMPHLETS.

WE'LL DANCE AROUND THE FIRE WITH RIGHTEOUS ABANDON AND CONTROLLED PASSION.

I'LL TAKE MY STAND AGAINST RACIST LIES...

YOU'LL TAKE YOURS AGAINST ABORTION...

AND IT WILL BE GREAT TO LIVE IN A COUNTRY WHERE BELIEF CAN BRING PEOPLE LIKE US TOGETHER.

© 1986 by P.S. Mueller. Reprinted by permission of *City Pages*, Minneapolis, Minnesota.

Sometimes all the books of a particular author are banned because some people find the author's ideas offensive. As the American Library Association points out, "No society of free men can flourish which draws up lists of writers to whom it will not listen, whatever they have to say."

Just because a library carries a certain book does not mean that the library endorses the views expressed by the author. It would be sad if libraries contained only books that the librarian liked and agreed with. One person's tastes and views should not be imposed on everyone else.

Libraries exist to promote learning. To fulfill this purpose, libraries must include works with different points of view and new ideas. The way to deal with ideas and words we hate is not to suppress them, but to think about them, discuss them, challenge them. As Supreme Court justice Louis Brandeis put it, "The fitting remedy for evil counsels is good ones." Libraries must be allowed to include both.

The author quotes the American Library Association, which has long been known for promoting "the freedom to read." Is this an effective testimonial? Why or why not?

Increased pressure on libraries

The author states that the pressure being placed on librarians to exclude certain books is harmful. Do you agree? Why or why not?

Evaluating Testimonials

Many speakers and writers quote or paraphrase the ideas of famous people and experts. They usually use these testimonials to add weight to their own argument. It is important to examine testimonials to see if they really do support the argument. Before beginning this activity, you may wish to reread the section on testimonials on page 5.

Below are several examples of testimonials. Evaluate each one and mark it according to the following code:

G for good use of a testimonial

P for poor use of a testimonial—for example, using a celebrity without consideration for his or her knowledge of the topic

I for irrelevant testimonial—one that has nothing to do with the topic under consideration

N for not a testimonial—a quotation that simply provides information, it does not present or support an opinion

Answers

1. According to the Library of Congress, thousands of new books are published each year. _____

2. The author and activist Phyllis Schlafly states, "The public has the right to exercise its right of free speech on how taxpayers' funds are spent and on what standards, to second-guess the judgement of the persons doing the spending, and to remove from office those responsible for any misuse of tax money." _____

3. Andrea Dworkin, a feminist author, says, "There are lots of people in this country, I am happy to say, who . . . will not accept the hatred of women as good, wholesome, American fun; they won't accept the hatred of women . . . as anybody's idea of freedom." _____

4. Christians say libraries should not carry books about the devil and witchcraft. _____

5. As the American Library Association points out, "No society of free men can flourish which draws up lists of writers to whom it will not listen, whatever they have to say." _____

PREFACE: Should Song Lyrics Be Censored?

In 1990, a Florida prosecuting attorney, Jack Thompson, asked U.S. District Court judge José Gonzales to decide whether an album by the rap group 2 Live Crew was obscene. Gonzales ruled that it was. Following the ruling, record stores were told to withdraw the record from their shelves. One record store owner, Charles Freeman, refused to do so. He continued to sell the record until an undercover police officer purchased a copy from his store. Freeman was arrested, and a jury found him guilty of selling obscene material.

Many people in the recording industry were shocked by Charles Freeman's conviction and many began to speak out on the issue. Music critic and biographer Dave Marsh formed the organization Right to Rock Network to fight music censorship. Editorials by record company executives appeared in newspapers across the country, criticizing the Freeman verdict.

Critics of the music industry argued that the 2 Live Crew case was not due to increasing censorship, but to increasing obscenity in music. They pointed out that the obscenity laws used to prosecute Charles Freeman had existed for years and that the Supreme Court had found these laws to be constitutional. What was new, these critics said, was that rock music lyrics were becoming so offensive that, for the first time, they met the Supreme Court's test for obscene speech.

The Court's test for obscenity was established in the 1973 case, *Miller v. California*. The Court said that speech could be considered obscene if it met a three-part test. First, the speech must be "patently offensive"; that is, it must offend a reasonable person's standards of decency. Second, it must appeal to a "shameful or morbid interest in sex." Third, it must be "lacking in serious social value." The Court left the finding of obscenity up to local juries on a case-by-case basis.

In 1992, a U.S. Court of Appeals overturned Judge Gonzales's ruling on the 2 Live Crew album. The appeals court said that the state of Florida did not prove the third criterion for obscenity: that the record lacked serious social value.

The debate over lyrics rages on. In 1992, the Simon Wiesenthal Center called for a boycott of Madonna's "Justify Your Love" album because they believed it expressed hatred toward Jews. Later in the year, police associations called for a boycott of Time Warner Inc. for promoting Ice-T's song "Cop Killer," which the officers said encouraged violence toward police.

The following viewpoints debate whether song lyrics should be censored.

Editor's Note: Recently, law enforcement officials have used obscenity laws to try to keep certain records out of their communities. In this viewpoint, the author uses this as an example to argue that the First Amendment was designed to stop these kinds of actions. The author quotes many experts to prove his point that records should not be censored. Are these testimonials persuasive?

Which propaganda technique does the author use in this paragraph?

Which propaganda techniques are used in this paragraph?

The author quotes an attorney who is paid to work for the music industry. Is this a useful testimonial? Why or why not?

Rock music censorship is nothing new. In the 1950s, the Ku Klux Klan burned the records of Chuck Berry, Little Richard, and others because they said it was corrupting white youth. People who do this are like Nazis. They are the same people who burn books. They must be stopped.

The founders of our nation tried to stop them. They said, "Congress shall make no law abridging . . . freedom of speech." This was not good enough for some people, who continue to crowd our courts with attempts to limit free speech. They use decency and obscenity laws to harass groups, such as 2 Live Crew, whom they hate. As Luther Campbell, the leader of 2 Live Crew argues, "There's a new breed of sheriff turning the music industry upside down. A few right-wing individuals have appointed themselves judge and jury for what's right and wrong."

The main reason given for placing limits on speech is to protect citizens. The question is, Who is being protected when a record like 2 Live Crew's "As Nasty As They Wanna Be" is banned? Not the two million people who bought the record. They enjoy it. Not the people who did not buy the record. They never heard it. John T. Mitchell, an

attorney for the recording industry says, "The only people served by the law are those who are offended at the thought that someone, somewhere, sometime, might enjoy reading, looking at or listening to such speech."

This is always the case with censors. They want to place limits on others. This is wrong. People should be able to decide for themselves what their moral standards will be. They do not need to be protected from themselves. Charles Edward Pogue, a screenwriter whose film credits include "The Fly," "Psycho III," and "DOA," put it this way, "I'm an intelligent, college-educated, fairly literate human being who's perfectly capable of making up his own mind. I don't need to be told what to read or see, be told how to interpret it or be told what to think. Lighten up and get off my back."

No words are so vile that they can harm anyone. The author Jamaica Kincaid told students at Dunbar High School in Washington, D.C., "No word can hurt you. None. No idea can hurt you. Not being able to express an idea or word will hurt you much more. As much as a bullet."

Kincaid is right. The danger lies in limiting expression. The minute we allow the government to say that some records are obscene and cannot be sold, we make it easier for the government to silence other artists. As Luther Campbell says, "Today they're trying to censor rap and tomorrow it could be classical music or theater or . . ."

Who knows, maybe your own thoughts and words will be next.

The word "always" is a clue that a propaganda technique is being used. Which one is it?

Is Mr. Pogue an appropriate person to provide a testimonial on this topic? Why or why not?

Are any propaganda techniques used in this paragraph? Name them.

Who is being protected?

The author says obscenity laws do not protect the people who buy obscene records, because they enjoy the songs. Do you agree or disagree? Who else might be protected by these laws?

Editor's Note: The author of this viewpoint argues that obscene song lyrics have a negative effect on society. These lyrics, the author says, can be banned for the same reason that other obscene materials have been banned in the past. As he did in the previous viewpoint, the author again uses many testimonials in this viewpoint. Decide whether these testimonials are useful or distracting.

Steve Kelley. Reprinted with permission.

The author includes several testimonials toward the end of this viewpoint. Do they support his argument? Explain.

According to the FBI, violent crimes are increasing. Rapes are up. Hate crimes are up. Attacks on police officers are up. Something is wrong with our society. We search our souls to find the answer. We look at government policies. We look at schools. We look at our families. But when we look at the messages that bombard us from televisions, radios, and boom boxes, we are told to look elsewhere. "The song isn't going to make somebody murder anyone," says the singer Ice-T about his record "Cop Killer." "I'm exercising free speech," he claims.

It is odd that writers of any kind, including songwriters, would argue that words have no effect—good or bad—on people, especially young people. It is odd and it is absurd. Clearly, words shape lives and influence history. The American Revolution would have happened anyway, but it happened at the precise moment it did in part because essays like Tom Paine's "Common Sense" urged it. If words have no effect, why do so many governments around the world censor speech and the press? Why do writers write? Why do singers sing?

Haven Bradford Gow, a columnist for *Conservative Review*, comments, "Common sense tells us that just as the great music of Handel, Haydn, Bach, Beethoven, Mozart, Vivaldi and Wagner can educate, enlighten, and inspire, the music and lyrics of all too many rock songs can corrupt by glamorizing and encouraging self- and socially-destructive behavior."

The Supreme Court believes in the power of words. That is why it limits certain forms of harmful speech. One of these forms of speech is obscene speech. The reason for limiting it is simple. As Warren Burger, former Supreme Court chief justice of the United States expressed it, "Why do we have laws against obscenity? For the same reason that we do not let people vent garbage into the street."

The jury in Fort Lauderdale, Florida, that convicted Charles Freeman of obscenity charges for selling "As Nasty As They Wanna Be" did so because they wanted to keep 2 Live Crew's rhyming garbage off their streets. The jury was well within its rights according to the Supreme Court. "There are legitimate state interests at stake in stemming the tide of commercialized obscenity," wrote the Court in the landmark case *Paris Theater v. Slaton*. "There is a 'Right of the Nation and of the States to maintain a decent society.'"

People in the music industry seem to believe they are exempt from the laws that govern motion pictures, books, magazines, and other forms of expression. Luther Campbell of 2 Live Crew argues that "the government has no power to restrict expression because of its message, its ideas, its subject matter or its content. So what's the problem?"

The problem is that Campbell does not understand constitutional law. He does not realize that tons of obscene material is banned each year because of its content. This is not dangerous. Obscene material, by definition, lacks serious ideas. "To equate the free and robust exchange of ideas and political debate with the commercial exploitation of obscene material . . . is a misuse of the great guarantees of free speech and free press," said the Supreme Court in 1973 in *Miller v. California*.

Limits on speech are not the only answer to America's problems, but they are part of the answer. It is time we stopped pretending otherwise.

What propaganda technique is being used in this paragraph?

Ramirez/Copley News Service. Reprinted with permission.

Rhyming trash

The author of this viewpoint says that obscene song lyrics are "rhyming garbage" that "lack serious value." He says these lyrics should be banned. Do you agree or disagree? Explain your answer.

Identifying Propaganda Techniques in Editorial Cartoons

Throughout the book, you have seen cartoons that illustrate the ideas in the viewpoints. Editorial cartoons are an effective and usually humorous way of presenting an opinion on an issue. Cartoonists sometimes use generalizations in their cartoons. That is, they imply that the idea presented by the cartoon is always the case.

Look at the cartoon below. Who are the people on the jury? What generalization is the cartoonist making about juries that decide obscenity cases? What does the cartoon imply about the obscenity laws themselves? Does the cartoonist think the verdicts in obscenity trials can be fair?

For further practice, look at the editorial cartoons in your daily newspaper. Try to decide if the cartoonist is generalizing about a subject in the cartoon.

A jury to decide obscenity laws.

Paul Conrad, © 1990, *Los Angeles Times.* Reprinted with permission.

FOR FURTHER READING

The author recommends the following books and periodicals for further research on the topic. Check the works consulted list that follows for further suggestions.

John Bull, "Freedom of Speech: Can It Survive?" *Vital Speeches of the Day*, December 1, 1991.

Stephen Chapman, "First Amendment Protects Opposing Views," *Conservative Chronicle*, July 8, 1992.

Christian Century, "2 Live Crew's Rap: Sex, Race, and Class," January 2-9, 1991.

Barbara Dority, "The War on Rock and Rap Music," *Humanist*, September/October 1990.

Terry Eastland, "Against Her Will," *The American Spectator*, July 1991.

Marjorie Heins, "Why Boycotting Booksellers Is a Bad Idea," *On the Issues*, Fall 1991.

Nat Hentoff, "People Who Actually, Truly, Believe in Freedom of Speech," *Liberal Opinion*, May 23, 1992.

Nat Hentoff, "Saving Kids from Satan's Books," *The Progressive*, May 1991.

John Leland, "Cube on Thin Ice," *Newsweek*, December 2, 1991.

John Leo, "A Sensible Judgment on Hate," *U.S. News & World Report*, July 6, 1992.

John Leo, "Our Misguided Speech Police," *U.S. News & World Report*, April 8, 1991.

Anthony Lewis, "Staving Off the Silencers," *The New York Times Magazine*, December 1, 1991.

Samuel Lipman, "Can We Save Culture," *National Review*, August 26, 1991.

John Underwood, "How Nasty Do We Wanna Be?" *Reader's Digest*, January 1991.

Phyllis Zagano, "Beyond the First Amendment: Censorship, Art, and Moral Responsibility," *Vital Speeches of the Day*, August 1, 1991.

WORKS CONSULTED

The following books and periodicals were used in the compilation of this book.

American Civil Liberties Union, *Why the American Civil Liberties Union Defends Free Speech for Racists and Totalitarians*, 1978. The ACLU explains why only a strict interpretation of the First Amendment will ensure that all voices are heard.

The American Library Association, "Freedom to Read" statement adopted June 25, 1953; revised January 28, 1972.

Robert Brannon, "Torturing Women As Fine Art: Why Some Women & Men are Boycotting Knopf," *On the Issues*, Fall 1991. A psychologist specializing in sex role research discusses the boycott of Knopf-Random House as a response to the publication of *American Psycho* by Bret Easton Ellis.

David S. Broder, "The Grave Danger in Press Ban," *San Diego Tribune*, November 11, 1984. The columnist argues that barring the press from military maneuvers could lead to a government monopoly of information.

Edwin A. Burtt, ed., *The English Philosophers from Bacon to Mill*. New York: Random House, Inc., 1939. An anthology of philosophic writings, including John Locke's "An Essay Concerning the True Origin, Extent, and End of Civil Government."

Luther Campbell, "Today They're Trying to Censor Rap, Tomorrow . . .," *Los Angeles Times*, November 5, 1990. The owner of Luke Records and leader of the rap group 2 Live Crew defends his recordings as an expression of his culture.

Mario M. Cuomo, "Preserving Freedom of the Press," *USA Today*, January 1988. The governor of New York argues that the press deserves absolute freedom.

Richard Conviser et al., *California II Bar/Bri Bar Review*. San Diego: Harcourt Brace Jovanovich, Inc., 1988. Provides an overview of constitutional law.

Haven Bradford Gow, "Heavy Metal Rock, Rap Music Lyrics, and the First Amendment," *Conservative Review*, October 1990. The columnist maintains that some contemporary lyrics have a corrupting influence on listeners.

Nat Hentoff, *The First Freedom*. New York: Delacorte Press, 1988. The author provides an overview of important First Amendment rulings.

Carlton Larson, "Should First Amendment Rights Be Unlimited?" Speech delivered before the City Club of Cleveland, December 12, 1991. The winner of a national high-school essay contest discusses the legal limits of free speech.

Lynn Marie Latham, "All Stories Send Out Messages, Intended or Not," *Los Angeles Times*, August 26, 1992. The co-creator and co-executive producer of ABC's "Homefront" television series discusses the need to balance good storytelling with an awareness for the negative cultural impact of story elements.

John Leo, "Polluting Our Popular Culture," *U.S. News & World Report*, July 2, 1990. The columnist maintains that rock music influences those who listen to it, which makes songs that glorify the abuse of women dangerous.

Los Angeles Times, "A Clumsy Law Out of the Very Best Motives," December 6, 1991. The editors discuss flaws in the St. Paul hate crime ordinance.

John C. Merrill, "Needed: An Ethical Press," *The World & I*, February 1988. A former reporter and editor argues that the power of the press must be limited because journalists are unethical and the public does not need to know certain government secrets.

Clarence Page, "Today 2 Live Crew! Tomorrow This Column?" *Liberal Opinion*, June 25, 1990. The columnist contends that while some song lyrics are sexist, there is no proof that they promote violence against women.

Charles Edward Pogue, "Don't Tell Me What to Read, See or Think," *Los Angeles Times*, 1991. The screenwriter responds to the growing number of protests, boycotts, and book bannings.

Phyllis Schlafly, "Citizens' Bill of Rights About Schools and Libraries," *The Phyllis Schlafly Report*, February 1983. The writer and political activist contends that those who spend taxpayer money on library books are accountable to the public for their selections.

Elmo R. Zumwalt and James G. Zumwalt, "Putting Responsibility Back into Journalism, *Conservative Chronicle*, October 4, 1989. The authors contend that the First Amendment should not be interpreted strictly because the Constitution's authors could not have known how powerful, and therefore dangerous, the press would become.

Accuracy in Media (AIM)
1275 K St. NW, Suite 1150
Washington, DC 20005
(202) 371-6710

AIM is a conservative watchdog organization. It researches public complaints on errors of fact made by the news media and requests that the errors be corrected publicly. It publishes the bimonthly *AIM Report* and a weekly syndicated newspaper column.

American Civil Liberties Union (ACLU)
132 W. 43rd St.
New York, NY 10036
(212) 944-9800

The ACLU champions the rights set forth in the Declaration of Independence and the Constitution. It opposes censoring any form of speech. The ACLU publishes the quarterly newsletter *Civil Liberties Alert* and several handbooks, public policy reports, project reports, civil liberties books, and pamphlets on the Freedom of Information Act.

American Library Association (ALA)
50 E. Huron St.
Chicago, IL 60611
(312) 944-6780

The ALA supports intellectual freedom and free access to libraries and library materials. The ALA's affiliated offices are the Office for Intellectual Freedom and Freedom to Read Foundation, which work for the legal and financial defense of intellectual freedom. The ALA publishes *Censorship, Litigation, and the Schools*, pamphlets, articles, audiovisual aids, and the annotated bibliography "Pressure Groups and Censorship."

Fund for Free Expression
36 W. 44th St.
New York, NY 10036
(212) 840-9460

This organization is a collection of journalists, writers, editors, publishers, and concerned citizens who work to preserve intellectual freedom throughout the world. It serves as the U.S. sponsor for the British publication *Index on Censorship*, which reports on violations of free expression. It publishes *Americas Watch Report.*

National Coalition Against Censorship (NCAC)
2 W. 64th St.
New York, NY 10023
(212) 724-1500

NCAC is an alliance of organizations committed to defending freedom of thought, inquiry, and expression by engaging in public education and advocacy on national and local levels. Their publications include *Censorship News* and *Report on Book Censorship Litigation in Public Schools.*

Parents' Music Resource Center (PMRC)
1500 Arlington Blvd., Suite 300
Arlington, VA 22209
(703) 527-9466

The PMRC was founded in 1985 to encourage placing warning labels on records with lyrics that promote sex, violence, and drug use. The center opposes censorship and instead calls for record companies to voluntarily print lyrics on the outside of record albums and to use a warning label on any album with explicit lyrics. It publishes the quarterly newsletter *The Record.*

INDEX